CAPTAIN
JOHN SMITH

CAPTAIN
JOHN SMITH

Henry Ira Kurtz

A Visual Biography

Illustrated with authentic prints and maps

Franklin Watts / New York / London / 1976

Historical consultant,
Professor Frederick Kershner, Jr.,
Teachers College, Columbia University

The photograph opposite the title page shows a statue of Captain John Smith at Jamestown, Virginia, commemorating his courageous adventures in the founding of the Jamestown colony.

Original maps and drawings by William K. Plummer
Photo research by Selma Hamdan
Cover design by Rafael Hernandez

Library of Congress Cataloging in Publication Data

Kurtz, Henry Ira.
　　Captain John Smith.

　　(A Visual biography)
　　Includes bibliographies and index.
　　SUMMARY: A biography of John Smith including his life before he voyaged to Virginia, but with special emphasis on his exploits in North America.
　　1. Smith, John, 1580–1631—Juvenile literature.
[1. Smith, John, 1580–1631. 2. Explorers] I. Title.
E229.S73　　973.2′1′0924 [B] [92]　　75-20148
ISBN 0-531-01105-4

A Note on the Illustrations

Many of the illustrations in this book are from early editions of Captain John Smith's own works. His early experiences in the fight against the Ottoman Turks are depicted by engravings from the 1630 edition of *The True Travels, Adventures, and Observations of Captaine John Smith*. The imaginative engravings of his adventures in Virginia are from the 1626 edition of *The Generall Historie of Virginia, New-England, and the Summer Isles*. In utilizing two photographs of Jamestown, Virginia, today we hope to show how history continues to live.

The original maps done for this book by William Plummer are indicated by the initials WKP.

Illustration credits

For my mother and father

LAND HO!

To the passengers and sailors on board the three small English ships, the first glimpse of the North American shoreline was a welcome sight indeed. Months had passed since their little fleet had sailed from England. During that time they had suffered every possible discomfort. Tossed about by stormy seas, plagued by seasickness, forced to live in cramped and filthy quarters, they had reached the point of despair. Sixteen days earlier they had left the West Indies on the last leg of their journey. They were bound for the land called Virginia, named in honor of England's "Virgin Queen" Elizabeth I, where they hoped to plant an English colony in the New World. Along the way, however, the flotilla had run into another furious storm. It seemed impossible that the ships would stay afloat. But luck and good seamanship had brought them through safely.

Now, after days of aimless wandering, their prayers were answered. At about 4 A.M. on the morning of April 26, 1607, the lookout cried out, "Land ho!" Before them, in the pre-dawn light, was the shadowy coastline of Virginia. Shouts of joy were given by those crowded along the rails. As they sailed into Chesapeake Bay, the sun rose to reveal sights that excited the weary, spray-soaked voyagers. Virginia in springtime blossomed like a true Garden of Eden. George Percy, one of the passengers, reported later—in the quaint English of the time—that they saw "faire meadows and goodly tall trees, with . . . fresh waters running through the woods."

Jubilation was clearly in order. But not everyone was happy. Among those who eagerly looked out at the sun-drenched woodlands was a short, bushy-bearded man with a proud, military bearing. His name was John Smith, and he had earned a reputation for courage and daring as a soldier fighting against the Turks in Europe. By rank he was a captain; and by virtue of heroic deeds performed on the battlefield he had the right to call himself an "English gentleman." Captain Smith did not join in the general gaiety on that pleasant spring day in 1607. Most likely he was in a sullen mood. During the long voyage from England he had been accused of plotting a mutiny and placed under arrest. He had narrowly escaped being hanged, and the charges still hung over him like a dark cloud.

Who was this Captain John Smith? What sort of man was he? To his admirers he was a brave and gallant soldier; a true hero whose leadership saved an English colony in America from disaster; a remarkable man of many talents. But while many applaud him, others take an opposite view. John Smith was a vain and arrogant man, his critics maintain. He was a power-hungry opportunist, a ruthless dictator—and a champion liar. As one scholar put it, "John Smith is one of those persons about whom historians are apt to lose their tempers." But even his harshest critics would agree that he was an extraordinary individual. Soldier, adventurer, colonist, explorer, author, and historian, John Smith lived many lives rolled into one.

Nearly every American is familiar with the famous story of how the Indian maiden Pocahontas saved John Smith from death. It is a part of American folklore. But John Smith deserves to be remembered for more important reasons. For, as we shall see,

Captain Smith played a key role in opening up the New World to English settlement. To understand how this complex man became one of America's most famous heroes we must go back to the days of his youth—to the England of Queen Elizabeth I.

THE SON OF A "POOR TENANT"

John Smith was born on January 9, 1580, in the small country village of Willoughby, in Lincolnshire, England. He was the first-born son of George Smith, a tenant farmer who rented his land from Lord Willoughby, a local nobleman for whom the town was named. Three other children were born to George Smith: a son named Francis in 1581, and a set of twins, Richard and Alice, in 1586. Richard, however, died ten days after his birth.

In later years John Smith would refer to himself as the son of a "poor tenant" farmer. He did this in order to show how he had risen from humble origins to a higher position. Actually, John's father was fairly well off. He had a comfortable home, and his land and possessions were worth a goodly sum for that day. Nevertheless, while the Smiths were far from poor, George Smith was not considered a "gentleman." Like other European nations, England was a class-conscious society. But John Smith was born in the midst of the Elizabethan Age, when the old order was beginning to crumble. Many eager and ambitious young men were making their mark; for the reign of Queen Elizabeth I was a period when Englishmen were inspired to perform brave deeds and produce great art.

Good Queen Bess, as Elizabeth was known, brought out the best in Englishmen. In the words of historian Will Durant, "she raised their courage to high enterprise, their minds to brave thinking, their manners to grace and wit and the fostering of poetry, drama, and art."

When Elizabeth became queen in 1558, England was a second-rate nation. The government was bankrupt; there was widespread poverty. But under her guidance, businessmen and merchants prospered; poverty was reduced. As British exports brought in large profits, merchants were able to invest money in overseas ventures to expand trade. For most of Elizabeth's reign there was peace, although English "sea dogs" like Sir Francis Drake and Sir John Hawkins carried on an undeclared naval war with Spain. In 1588, these hardy seamen defeated a great fleet—the Spanish Armada—which had been sent to conquer England by King Philip II of Spain. When Queen Elizabeth died in 1603, her kingdom had become one of the most powerful nations of Europe—and a match for Spain, England's main rival on the high seas.

It was during this glorious age in England that John Smith grew to manhood. But for an English farm boy there was little glory or excitement. Mostly it was just hard work. As the oldest son, young John performed his share of farm chores. Besides planting and harvesting crops and tending to livestock, there were many other tasks. John probably helped his father weave reeds into baskets and carve spoons, bowls, and other household items out of wood.

Elizabeth I of England.
A painting by
Marcus Gheeraerts.

Although he learned much that would be useful to him later as a colonist in Virginia, John disliked farming. Of course, he also attended school. Until he was seven John went to the local free grammar school at Alford, about four miles from his home. A thirst for adventure grew in John even as a boy. He read stories of the knights of the Middle Ages and dreamed of performing heroic acts. While others settled into routine lives as tradesmen, farmers, and men of commerce, John thought only of a life of action. His mind "even then being set on brave adventures," as he later wrote, he sold his school books in order to have money to run off to sea. But John's father learned of his son's plans and prevented him from leaving. At the higher grammar school he attended, he was taught Latin and "good manners and polite literature."

When he was fifteen, John was apprenticed to Thomas Sendall, a prosperous merchant in the town of King's Lynn. The life of an apprentice was hard, with long hours and low pay. With his rebellious nature, John was like a dog on a leash straining to break free. Each day he saw ships coming from the continent of Europe, sails and pennants snapping in the breeze. He could smell the fresh sea air and he yearned to travel, to see the world.

In 1596, John's father died, and soon after, his mother remarried. Now John no longer felt obligated to remain at home. He asked his master, Thomas Sendall, for permission to leave, as was required by law. When that was refused, he daringly took off on his own. It was only one of many acts of rebellion against authority during his reckless career. John went to Holland, where he joined a company of soldiers commanded by an English officer. For the next three years he fought against Spanish troops who were trying to conquer Holland.

Eventually, John made his way back to England. He was nineteen and still trying to find his way in life; and so he became what we would now call a "dropout." He went off into the woods to live alone, taking with him a horse and a lance. In his forest retreat—when he wasn't practicing horsemanship or hunting for deer—John had time to think about his future. He began to read books about warfare and soldiering. John's boyhood fantasy of becoming a knight had stayed with him. But with the passing of feudalism, knighthood had faded away. Soldiering was the closest thing to knighthood in John Smith's time. And so he decided to become a soldier—a modern knight errant.

OFF TO
THE WARS

But upon what field of glory was our young hero to perform his brave deeds? England was at peace. Fortunately, there was plenty of work for soldiers of fortune across the English Channel on the European continent. The Ottoman Turks, whose armies had conquered the Middle Eastern lands and much of North Africa, had also overrun parts of southern Europe. By 1600, these fierce Muslim warriors had reached Hungary. There Christians and Turks battled for control of central Europe.

A true Christian "knight," John Smith set off in 1600 to fight against the "heathen Turks." What we know about Smith during these years comes from his book of memoirs, *The True Travels, Adventures, and Observations of Captaine John Smith*. Smith was only twenty years of age when he left England. He was a short man, a little over five feet in height. But he was sturdily built, with a muscular and athletic body.

Smith arrived in Graz, Austria, in the summer of 1601. Graz was the headquarters of the Christian forces of the Holy Roman Empire. (The empire included land that is now present-day Germany, Austria, Switzerland, the Netherlands, and parts of other European countries.) In Graz, Smith was befriended by an English Jesuit priest who introduced him to "gentlemen of good quality." Among these was Baron Hanns Khisl, a high-ranking officer. Khisl was impressed by the young Englishman's knowledge of military matters. Smith was assigned to a Hungarian regiment commanded by Colonel Henry Folta, the Earl of Meldritch.

Smith first saw action against the Turks at the siege of Oberlimbach, a fortified town in the part of Hungary still controlled by the Christian forces. A Turkish army had surrounded the city. Baron Khisl's force, including Smith's regiment, was sent to lift the siege. But Khisl had a problem. How could he get a message to the troops in Oberlimbach that he was ready to attack? Smith had an idea. The commander of Oberlimbach was an officer Smith had met in Graz. The Englishman remembered telling the officer about a system of using signal lights to send messages.

Smith's suggestion saved the day. Khisl used torches to signal the commander of Oberlimbach that he would attack at a given time. The besieged garrison was then to launch its own attack on the Turks. To throw the Turks off guard, Smith came up with another clever tactic. Several thousand pieces of lighted fuse were set up to look like a division of musketeers. The ruse worked. While the Turks turned their guns toward the dummy

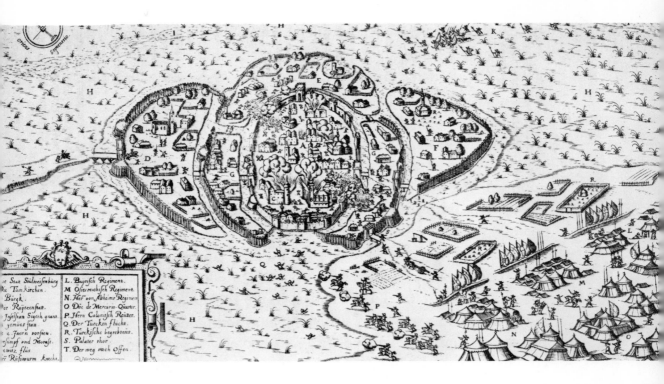

*The liberation of Stuhlweissenburg,
Hungary, in September 1601. An
engraving from* Ortelius Redivivus
by Hieronymus Ortelius, 1665.

army, Baron Khisl and his troops charged from another direction.
At the same time, according to plan, the garrison of Oberlimbach
came swarming out. Caught between the two forces, the Turks
panicked and fled.

As a reward for his good work, Smith was given a sum of
money and the rank of captain. He was put in charge of a force of
cavalry in the Earl of Meldritch's regiment. Smith fought in a
number of battles during the final months of 1601. In Decem-

ber, a force of 6,000 men commanded by the Earl of Meldritch, and including Smith, was sent to Transylvania—the eastern part of the kingdom of Hungary (which was then an independent principality).

There, Meldritch joined forces with Prince Sigismund Bathory, the local ruler, who was trying to defend his people from attacks by a ruthless band of mercenaries called the Hajdus (pronounced High-doos). The Hajdus were a mixture of Turks, Hungarians, and Tartars. For months these "bandits" and "renegades," as Smith called them, had been terrorizing the local population. Towns were looted and burned; thousands of innocent civilians were slaughtered.

In an effort to put an end to these cutthroats, Meldritch's troops pursued them across the rugged, mountainous terrain. Finally, the Hajdus took refuge in a fortified city. Sigismund's army, commanded by General Moses Szekely, and Meldritch's troops laid siege to the town. Secure behind their strong walls, the Hajdus were confident they could resist any attack. But after a few weeks they became restless. A Turkish *bashi* (officer) sent out a challenge. To provide some amusement, he would fight a duel to the death with any Christian officer who held the rank of captain or higher. The winner would claim the head and armor of the loser.

This was just the opportunity for fame and glory Captain Smith was looking for. A duel on horseback, mounted and in full armor—just like the knights of old he had read about as a boy! Smith was eager for the chance to make a name for himself. However, others in his camp also wanted to cross swords with the Turkish warrior. Lots were drawn and Smith won.

On the appointed day, the rival knights entered the field and took their positions. A trumpet sounded the charge and the two men galloped toward each other. Soldiers on both sides fell silent as the two horsemen closed the gap between them. As the two warriors met in a swirl of dust, Smith drove his lance through the Turk's face mask and into his head. The enemy nobleman tumbled dead from his mount.

Quickly dismounting, Smith removed the fallen Hajdu's helmet and cut off his head. He then presented the gory trophy to General Szekely, "who kindly accepted it." A second Turk now offered to fight Smith "to regain his friend's head or lose his own." The Englishman won another easy victory and then cockily issued a challenge of his own. He would duel with any Hajdu officer of equal rank with the slain Turks. A third duel was fought and Smith again emerged victorious.

With great fanfare, his jubilant comrades escorted him to General Szekely, bringing with them the three Turks' heads impaled on lances. The general warmly embraced Smith and presented him with a fine horse and a jeweled scimitar (a curved sword used by Turks and Arabs). While Smith was fighting his duels, Szekely had used the time to mount his heavy artillery on a sixty-foot-high earthwork. After battering the enemy walls for two weeks, the Christian troops stormed the city and captured it.

Shortly after this victory, Prince Sigismund arrived to review his troops. When he learned of Captain Smith's exploits, Sigismund awarded him a coat of arms. This was a high honor generally given only to those who performed great deeds of valor. Smith was authorized to "design and impress upon his shield three Turks' heads." In addition, Sigismund appointed Smith "an English gentleman"—which he had no legal right to do—and granted him an annual pension of 300 ducats (about $4,000).

Smith later participated in other campaigns. His last was at

om hee releeued OLVMPAGH by a stratagem of lights Chap 4

His Combat with GRVALGO Capt of three hundred horsmen

Three TVRK'S heads in a banner giuen him for Armes

pro Christo Patria

Sigismundus

How he was presented to Prince SIGISMVNDVS. Chap 8.

a place called Rotenthurn near the Altus River. The badly out-numbered European troops were overwhelmed by the Tartars.* Meldritch and about fourteen hundred cavalrymen tried to escape by fording the river. Many of them drowned or were killed by Tartar arrows. Smith was wounded in the battle and enemy sol-diers looting the dead took him prisoner. He was carried to Axio-polis, a city on the Danube River, and sold as a slave. A rich Turk bought him as a gift for a Turkish noblewoman. With other slaves, Smith was transported to Constantinople, capital of the vast Ottoman Turkish Empire. Chained to each other in groups of twenty, the slaves had to travel the last 140 miles of the journey on foot. Exhausted and half-starved, they plodded along until they finally reached the city.

Smith was taken directly to the home of the Turkish noble-woman, whose name he gives as Charatza. While in her home he was well treated. Unfortunately, Charatza had no use for a slave. She sent the Englishman to her brother, who was a Timor (a petty military chieftain) in a region north of the Caucasus Mountains, in what is now Russia. Smith's new master turned out to be a

Above, signal torches were used to communicate with the army within Oberlimbach. An engraving from The True Travels, Adventures, and Observations *of Captain John Smith,* London, 1630. Center, John *Smith accepting the challenge of the Turkish warrior. An engraving from* True Travels, 1630. Below, *John Smith returning in triumph with the three Turks' heads. An engraving from* True Travels, 1630.

* Wild, nomadic warriors from Central Asia who were allies of the Turks.

John Smith as he was sold into slavery.
An engraving from True Travels, *1630.*

cruel man. Life under the Timor was so bad, according to Smith, that "a dog could hardly have lived to endure."

During the harvest time in the fall of 1603, Smith was put to work in a storage hut a few miles from the Timor's castle. One afternoon, while the Englishman was threshing grain, his master came in and for no reason began to curse and beat him. By this time, Smith had taken all he could. He turned on his master and clubbed him to death with his threshing bat. Smith had thought often of escape, and now he had his chance. Stripping off the dead man's clothes, he put them on. Then he took the Timor's horse and rode off.

A long trip lay ahead of him. It was over one thousand miles of desert, rugged mountains, and dense forests. After many weeks of hard travel, he reached Transylvania and received a warm welcome from his comrades. From there he continued on to Germany, where he met Prince Sigismund. The prince enthusiastically greeted the brave English officer. He gave him a gift of 1,500 gold ducats and a document (dated December 9, 1603) confirming the earlier award of the coat of arms.

Following a series of minor adventures, including a brief trip to North Africa, Smith decided to return to England. But nothing ever came easily to John Smith. One of the ships he took passage on turned pirate and was nearly sunk when it attacked two innocent-looking ships that proved to be Spanish men-of-war. At last, late in 1604, he reached the familiar shores of his native land.

FACT OR FICTION?

If we are to believe what John Smith wrote in his *True Travels*, he had experienced—by the age of twenty-four—more thrills, excitement, and hairbreadth escapes than most men have in a lifetime. But did all of this really happen? Was Smith telling the truth when he wrote about his adventures more than twenty years later? Or are the stories in his *True Travels* the fantasies of a braggart and a liar? Generations of historians have argued about this. Some have stated flatly that John Smith was a liar. For many years most scholars took the position that Smith's *True Travels* was mainly romantic fiction mixed with a dash of fact.

The question of whether John Smith was or was not a liar is an important one. For if he lied about his exploits in Hungary, he may also have lied about his later adventures in Virginia. In the 1950s, a historian named Laura Polanyi Striker, who had been educated in Hungary, came forward to rescue Smith's reputation. With her knowledge of Hungarian, Dr. Striker was able to do what American historians could not. She could examine first-hand old manuscripts and records in the Hungarian archives.

After careful research, Dr. Striker concluded that in every instance where the facts could be checked, Smith's account was basically accurate and truthful. Summing up her findings, Dr. Striker wrote: "He [Smith] could not possibly have written as he did about Hungary without having lived through the events he described. It is time we give him credit for being not only a valiant fighter but an acute historian and chronicler as well."

Earlier historians were confused because they could find no record of names and events mentioned in Smith's *True Travels*. The problem was that Smith relied on his memory when giving the names of people and places. Thus Baron Khisl became "Kisell" and the city of Oberlimbach was written as "Olumpagh." His commander Colonel Folta was remembered as "Volda." There is nothing surprising about this. The English of that day were very casual about spelling. In Smith's case, he was spelling foreign names the way they sounded to him.

No doubt Smith exaggerated his exploits and added plenty of color and drama when writing about them. He may have been a braggart, but then he had a lot to brag about. Nevertheless, as Philip Barbour, a recent Smith biographer, has pointed out, ". . . nothing John Smith wrote has yet been found to be a lie."

HOME AGAIN

It was a much-changed John Smith who arrived in England after four years in foreign lands. He was no longer an awkward, starry-eyed farm boy and merchant's apprentice. Now he was a man, tested by combat and experienced in the ways of the world. Thus it was Captain John Smith, soldier, adventurer, and "gentleman," who sailed up the Thames River to London late in 1604.

Smith had come home with 1,500 ducats—a princely sum—jingling in his purse, and so he could afford the comforts of life. Most likely he took lodging in one of the city's many inns. No doubt Smith spent the first few months after his return enjoying the pleasures of England's capital and largest city.

But Smith was not the sort of man who could remain idle for long. His exploits in Europe and Central Asia had merely whetted his appetite for adventure. He had enough of the Old World, but across the ocean the New World beckoned. How exciting it would be to see for himself the forested wilderness of North America and the "savage" Indians he had heard about.

Just how and when Smith first became interested in the New World is not certain. But at some point he began to think of becoming an explorer and colonist. In London at that time, there were many prominent merchants and businessmen, as well as adventurers like himself, who were interested in establishing English colonies in North America. Possibly with the aid of friends among the aristocracy, Smith made contact with these people. There is evidence that he was involved in planning the expedition to Virginia that was to leave England at the end of 1606.

BACKGROUND
TO JAMESTOWN

Five years after Christopher Columbus discovered the New World in 1492, John Cabot planted England's flag on the coast of North America. The Cabot voyages (1497–1498) gave England a claim to a portion of the North American continent. However, the English were slow to take advantage of that claim. In the century that followed the voyages of Columbus and Cabot, Spain carved out a great empire in the New World. Other European nations began to explore the Americas, hoping to get their share of the new lands.

Yet no serious effort was made to found a permanent English colony in North America until the 1580s. By then many far-sighted Englishmen were arguing that England must take possession of North America before the Spaniards and others beat them to it. They predicted that overseas colonies would reduce unemployment at home, expand trade, and lessen England's dependence on foreign imports. Perhaps the colonists would discover gold, silver, or a passage to Asia.

In the 1580s, Sir Walter Raleigh and Sir Humphrey Gilbert made several unsuccessful attempts to plant colonies in North America. The colonization movement suffered a temporary setback because of these failures. But Queen Elizabeth had laid the groundwork for future colonies. Unfortunately, the war with Spain occupied the country's attention for many years. Businessmen found it more profitable to finance the English privateers that plundered Spanish treasure ships than to invest in colonies.

Following the death of Queen Elizabeth in 1603, James Stuart of Scotland came to the English throne as King James I. King James promptly signed a treaty of peace with Spain and promised to put an end to raids by English privateers. Businessmen now had to look elsewhere for quick riches. Once again their attention turned to the New World.

Groups of merchants interested in opening up new trade routes formed joint-stock corporations, which raised money by selling shares of stock to investors. In 1605, two of these groups, representing the cities of London and Plymouth, petitioned King James for permission to establish settlements in Virginia. Among the members of the London group were some of the most prominent backers of colonization. It was this group that Captain John Smith joined.

On April 10, 1606, King James issued a royal charter establishing two joint-stock companies—the Virginia Company of London (or London Company), and the Plymouth Company. The charter granted to "certain Knights, Gentlemen, Merchants and other Adventurers" of the two cities the right to plant colonies in "that part of *America,* commonly called Virginia." (At the time, Virginia was the name given to all of the North American territory claimed by the English.) Two zones were established. The Plymouth Company could found a colony in northern

19

King James I
of England.

Virginia, while the London Company could do the same in the southern part.

The Plymouth Company was the first to voyage forth. In August 1606, a ship was sent out and the following year a colony was established on the coast of Maine. But in 1608, following a severe winter, the settlement was abandoned. Meanwhile, the London Company began its own preparations. Stock was sold, money raised, and ships were obtained. By the end of 1606, the London Company had recruited a little over a hundred colonists, plus crews for the ships that would carry them. A few days before Christmas 1606, the voyagers boarded the vessels and sailed down the Thames. There were three ships. The largest was the *Susan Constant*,* commanded by Captain Christopher Newport, who would be in charge of the expedition until it reached Virginia. Newport carried with him a sealed box containing the names of the men who would form the council that governed the colony in Virginia. (The Virginia Council would in turn be responsible to the company's London Council appointed by the king.) The fleet also included two smaller ships: the *Godspeed*, under Captain Bartholomew Gosnold, and the *Discovery*, commanded by Captain John Ratcliffe.

Smith calculated that there were 105 men on board when the fleet set sail, but other sources give figures ranging from 93 to 154—of whom about 100 were to remain in Virginia. Who were these adventurers? And why had they chosen to leave their families and comfortable homes in England to risk their lives in the wilderness of North America? Fifty-nine of those whose names are known were listed as "gentlemen." They were mainly young aristocrats, such as George Percy, son of the Earl of Northumber-

* Also known as the *Sarah Constant*.

21

land. There were also some bricklayers and carpenters, a barber, a tailor, and a blacksmith. One clergyman, the Reverend Robert Hunt, and a doctor went along. The rest were soldiers and sailors.

Many of these men were driven by a lust for gold, silver, and other riches, for it was generally believed that Virginia was a land of unlimited wealth. But this was not the only reason. Some, like John Smith, went mainly for thrills and adventure. Others sought to escape the closed society of the Old World, where class prejudices were still strong. In the New World, it was thought, all men would be equals. A few, like the Reverend Hunt, felt they had a mission to convert the Indians to Christianity. "Gold, Glory and God" were the chief reasons these men had signed on.

VOYAGE TO VIRGINIA

The expedition got off to a bad start. No sooner did the ships enter the English Channel than stormy seas stopped them dead in their tracks. For nearly six weeks, the voyagers were forced to remain near the coast of England, crowded together in close quarters. Finally, early in February, the seas became calmer and the winds more favorable. The little fleet headed south, toward the Canary Islands, in order to follow the southern route to the West Indies used by Columbus.

The voyage was a long one, and by the time the ships reached the West Indies there was much grumbling among the members of the expedition. Tempers flared and arguments broke out. An outspoken man, Smith soon made enemies. He was openly critical of Edward Maria Wingfield and the other leaders. Smith and Wingfield took an instant dislike to each other. Wingfield was a high-born aristocrat and, in Smith's opinion, a pompous windbag. Wingfield and several of his fellow aristocrats, who considered the twenty-seven-year-old Smith a brash young upstart, accused him of planning a mutiny.

Smith stoutly denied the charge. But Captain Newport was persuaded that it was true and Smith was placed under arrest. According to Smith's account, he was first sentenced to death. Fortunately, Newport had a change of heart and simply ordered him placed in confinement for the rest of the voyage. For several weeks the fleet island-hopped through the West Indies, picking up fresh supplies and recovering from the long ocean voyage. Then the ships headed north.

Land was sighted on the morning of April 26, 1607. They had reached the mouth of the Chesapeake Bay, off the coast of Virginia. A small party of men, headed by Captain Newport, went ashore, landing on the southern cape (Cape Henry). As the group was returning to its boats, a band of Indians appeared. The Indians let loose a volley of arrows at the strange invaders, wounding two members of the party. The Englishmen replied by firing their muskets, and the Indians fled into the woods.

That night the sealed box containing the names of the seven councilors was opened. The list included Edward Maria Wingfield, George Kendall, John Martin, and the three ships' captains —Newport, Gosnold, and Ratcliffe. The seventh name on the list was Captain John Smith. Smith's enemies on the council were

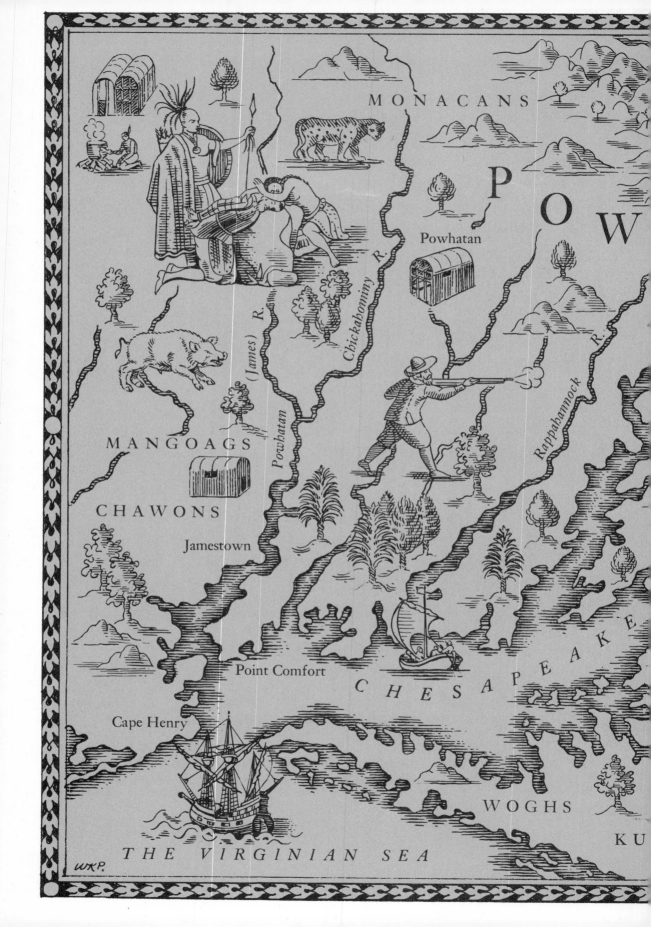

MONACANS

POW

Powhatan

Chickahominy R.

(James) R.

Powhatan

Rappahannock R.

MANGOAGS

CHAWONS

Jamestown

Point Comfort

CHESAPEAKE

Cape Henry

WOGHS

KU

THE VIRGINIAN SEA

WKP.

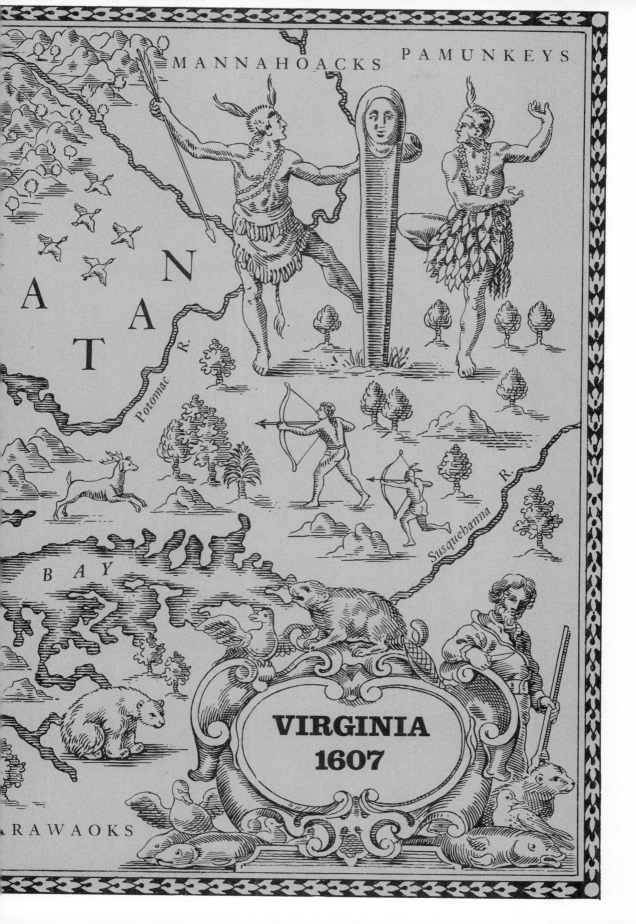

outraged. Regardless of the instructions, they were not going to let a troublemaker and know-it-all like Smith sit on the council. The young soldier was denied his place and kept under arrest.

Using a small sailboat called a shallop, Captain Newport and about twenty men spent the following days sailing up the James River (named in honor of the king). Along the way, the Englishmen were well received by various Indian tribes, who entertained them "with feasting, smoking huge pipes of tobacco, singing and dancing." Eventually, Newport and his party reported that they had found a suitable location for the settlement. The place selected was a small outcropping of land about sixty miles upriver from Chesapeake Bay. It was almost completely surrounded by water, which made it easy to defend. Because the river was quite deep at this point, their ships could sail up to the shore. On May 13, the ships arrived at what was to become known as Jamestown Island.*

Just as the river had been named for the king, so, too, was the new settlement. It was to be called "James Towne." During the night, the council was formally sworn in—all except Captain Smith—and Wingfield was elected president.

The morning of May 14, the colonists went ashore. Sixteen of those who had started the voyage had died along the way, but the rest were in good spirits as they started to build their new settlement. "Now falleth every man to work," noted Smith. The first few days were busy ones. A rough sketch of a fort was drawn up by the council members. Some men went to work cutting down trees and constructing crude wooden huts. Others planted wheat and vegetables or made nets for catching fish. Thus was born the first permanent English settlement in the New World.

---

* Actually, Jamestown was a peninsula connected to the mainland by a narrow isthmus, but it was designated Jamestown Island by its earliest settlers.

From the very outset, however, Smith was critical of the way the council was managing the infant colony. His soldier's instinct told him a sturdier fort should be built. He also wanted the men given regular military drill so the settlement would not be caught off guard if an attack came. But since he was an unrecognized member of the council, his pleas went unheeded. Yet Smith had good reason to be worried. The Indians might be friendly one minute, warlike the next.

On May 21, Newport and about twenty men set off in the shallop to explore upriver. Smith had apparently earned Newport's respect, for he was allowed to go with the explorers, even though still nominally under arrest. The colonists were under orders from the Virginia Company to look for gold and to try and find a water route to Asia. Newport's group cruised up the James as far as The Falls, near the present city of Richmond. During the trip, they picked up an Indian guide named Navirans, who taught Smith and his comrades Indian words. Smith had a knack for learning languages and in a matter of months could speak several Indian dialects. This knowledge was to prove useful in trading with the Indians later on.

Although the Indians had no gold or silver, the Englishmen found bits of rock that they thought might contain gold ore. At the end of May, the party returned to Jamestown. There they learned that the settlement had been attacked by Indians. A boy had been killed and another settler had died of wounds. About a dozen others had been injured. Now the council listened to Smith's pleas for better defenses. Work on the fort was pressed, while the colonists drilled under Smith's watchful eye.

When completed, the fort was laid out in the form of a triangle, with a palisade made of sharpened logs. At each corner of the triangle was a bulwark, or gun emplacement, shaped "like a half-moon." Several cannons were mounted on each of the bulwarks.

A church, a storehouse, and a few flimsy houses for the settlers had been built. Smith was the main architect of the defenses. Because of his work on the fort, Captain Newport and the Reverend Hunt requested that the charges against him be dropped. On June 10, he was formally admitted to the council.

Later that month, Newport sailed back to England, taking with him a cargo of wood, some sassafras roots—used to make drugs—and the rocks believed to contain gold. No sooner had Newport left than the colony fell on hard times. After the first flush of enthusiasm, many of the "gentlemen" aristocrats refused to do their share of work. They had come to plunder the land and get rich. Manual labor was beneath them, and they spent the days searching for gold. Instead of fishing or hunting for game, they preferred to live on the meager supply of food brought on the ships. Soon the ships' stores began to give out.

Worse was to come. When the settlers had arrived in Virginia, they had been deceived by the weather. May was a gentle, pleasant month. But in July and August the days became unbearably hot and humid. Nor had they paid attention to the mosquito-infested swamplands surrounding the island. Before long many of them were stricken by malaria. Others caught typhoid fever from contaminated water. Almost half of the colonists were dead by September. It appeared unlikely that the feeble colony would survive another month.

James Fort near Jamestown, Virginia, is a full-scale reconstruction of the palisaded fort built by the settlers in 1607.

CAPTAIN SMITH
SAVES THE COLONY

With sickness and starvation came despair. Quarrels broke out among the remaining settlers. President Wingfield was accused of bad leadership and of deliberately withholding food from the others. Finally Captain Smith and John Martin, the only surviving council members, removed him from office. Wingfield was placed under arrest and brought to trial. Later, he was sent back to England.

But hard work still remained. The colonists continued to suffer. Although John Ratcliffe took over as president, someone was needed to take charge of the everyday management of the colony. Smith stood out as a man who had the ability to organize and lead, and he was given the job. He immediately put the men to work, "some to mow, others to binde thatch; some to build houses, others to thatch them . . . so that in a short time he provided most of them lodgings, neglecting any for himselfe."

Food was urgently needed. With a small party of men, Smith sailed down the James to trade with the Indians. By hard bargaining and occasional threats of force, Smith got what he wanted. He returned to the colony with his boat loaded with fish, oysters, deer meat, bread, and sixteen bushels of corn. Other food-gathering expeditions followed this one. Smith's efforts undoubtedly saved Jamestown's settlers from starvation. Even Wingfield, Smith's bitter foe, admitted that the young soldier's trading voyages "relieved the colony well."

As summer turned to fall, the situation at Jamestown improved. Cooler weather replaced the terrible heat. Crops of corn, beans, and peas, planted earlier with the help of friendly Indians, began to sprout. Thanks to Smith and the Indians, the colony would be able to survive the coming winter.

In December, Smith sailed up the Chickahominy River in an effort to reach the village of Chief Powhatan, ruler of most of the Indian tribes in that part of Virginia. It was the beginning of a legendary adventure. Smith and a small party of men cruised up the winding river in a barge. When the river became too shallow for the barge, Smith continued on in a canoe with two of his men and two Indian guides. Farther upstream the group went ashore.

Leaving his men and one Indian behind, Smith and the other Indian entered the woods. While he was gone, a party of Pamunkey Indians attacked and killed his comrades. A few minutes later he and his guide were surrounded by several hundred painted warriors. Arrows came whizzing toward him. One struck him in the thigh; several others pierced his clothes. Using his Indian guide as a shield, Smith fought back, loading and firing his clumsy, muzzle-loading pistol as fast as he could.

Smith claimed that he killed three warriors and wounded several more. Because the Indians feared his pistol, he was able to hold them at a distance. But as he tried to make a run for it, he slipped and fell into a muddy creek. His feet became stuck in the mud and he could not move. It was a freezing winter day and his feet soon became numb from the cold. Seeing that he could not escape, Smith surrendered. The Indians pulled him out and took him to their chief, Opechancanough. As a token of friend-

Their triumph about him.

C. Smith bound to a tree to be shott to death
1607

A Coniurer.   Their   Idoll   A Preist

Their Coniuration ghout
C: Smith 1607

ship, Smith gave the chief a small compass. The gift won over the chief, who decided to keep Smith as a prisoner instead of killing him. He was "kindly feasted" and otherwise well treated by the Indians.

For several weeks, Smith was taken on a tour of Indian villages along the Rappahannock and Potomac rivers. Finally, the Englishman was brought to the village of Chief Powhatan. Two hundred warriors stood guard around Powhatan's lodge. They looked grimly at the white captive "as if he had been some monster." After Powhatan and his fellow chieftains had prepared themselves, Smith was led before them. Powhatan was seated at one end of the lodge on a throne made of piled mats. On either side of the lodge sat the ranking men of the tribe, with their women behind them.

Smith was clearly awed by the sight of the great chief, whom he described as "a tall, well-proportioned man, with a sour look." His expression was "grave and majestical," which was in keeping with his high station. For Powhatan was not merely a chief but an emperor who ruled a confederacy of more than twenty tribes and some eight thousand Indians.

At first Captain Smith's reception was friendly. He was greeted by "a great shout" and then treated to another lavish meal.

Captain Smith being taken prisoner, then bound to a tree to be shot to death. An engraving from The Generall Historie of Virginia, New-England, and the Summer Isles, *London, 1626 edition. Below, Captain Smith as a prisoner of the Indians. The priest and conjuror weave a spell about him. An engraving from* The Generall Historie of Virginia, *1626.*

But suddenly the situation changed. Following a conference by the chiefs, two heavy stones were brought in and placed before Powhatan. Warriors seized the bewildered Englishman and pushed his head down on the stones. War clubs were raised, and Smith was certain that he was about to have his head bashed in.

And then occurred one of the best-known incidents in American history. But let Captain Smith tell it in his own words. As the warriors prepared to deliver the death blows, Smith later recalled, "Pocahontas, the king's dearest daughter, when no entreaty could prevail, got his head in her arms, and laid her own upon his to save him from death. Whereat the Emperor was contented he should live. . . ."

It is a wonderful story, and one that is known by every American who has ever read a history book. But did it really take place? Over the years, historical opinion about the Pocahontas story has swung back and forth like a pendulum. In the beginning the story was generally thought to be true. Later it was denounced by Smith's critics as pure fiction. Today, most scholars believe the Pocahontas incident did occur, though perhaps not exactly as Smith wrote about it.

There is no doubt that Pocahontas actually lived. At the time of Smith's captivity, the Indian maid was twelve or thirteen years old. However, her real name was not Pocahontas; it was Matoaka. Her father nicknamed her "Pocahontas," * meaning "playful one."

But a question still remains. Why was Powhatan so easily swayed by his daughter's plea for mercy? After all, Smith had

---

* Pocahontas later married an English settler named John Rolfe. The Rolfes visited England in 1616 and the Indian princess was introduced at court to King James. On her way home to Virginia, in 1617, she fell ill and died. She was buried at Gravesend, England.

King Powhatan comands C. Smith to be slayne, his
daughter Pokahontas beggs his life his thankfullness
and how he Subiected 39 of their kings reade y hister

*Above, Captain Smith,
condemned to death, is
saved by the daughter of
Powhatan. An engraving
from* The Generall His-
torie of Virginia, *1626.
Right, Matoaka, or Poca-
hontas, took the name of
Rebecca when she was
baptized a Christian.*

Ætatis suæ 21. Æ.
1616.

killed three of his warriors and should have been executed. There are several possible answers. For one thing, Indian custom provided that if a woman of the tribe spoke up for a captive his life would be spared. Another good reason is that Smith was known to be a chief of the whites. If the Indians killed him, the English settlers at Jamestown might seek revenge. Powhatan was a wise leader. Rather than risk a war with the white men, who had muskets and cannons, he may have decided it was better to let Smith live.

Not long after the incident, Powhatan and some of his warriors took Smith to a house in the woods. There a ceremony was performed and the Englishman was adopted into the tribe. Powhatan told Smith that he would "forever esteem him as his son" and gave him the Indian name Nantaquoud. Then he allowed Smith to return to Jamestown, escorted by twelve Indian guides.

CAPTAIN NEWPORT RETURNS

Smith reached Jamestown in the early days of January 1608. More trouble awaited him. John Ratcliffe and Gabriel Archer accused Smith of being responsible for the deaths of the two colonists killed by the Indians. Smith was tried, convicted, and sentenced to be hanged. Before the sentence could be carried out, Captain Newport sailed up the James, bringing with him another 120 settlers, fresh supplies, and instructions from the London Council. Newport intervened on Smith's behalf and obtained his release.

Newport's arrival was indeed timely, for the colony as well as for Smith. Fewer than forty of the original settlers remained alive. In London, Newport had reported that "the country is excellent and very rich in gold and copper." But the rock samples he brought back contained no gold and the London Company's directors were disappointed. Fortunately, the cargo of timber and sassafras paid for the expense of the voyage. As a result, the colony's backers were persuaded that a source of profit might yet be found. Newport was sent back with orders to press the search for gold and the Northwest Passage to Asia.

Shortly after his return, another calamity struck. Fire swept through the settlement, destroying many of the buildings and part of the fort's defensive wall. Hasty repairs were made, but a full rebuilding program was not begun. Newport was more interested in following the company's instructions to search for gold. Smith believed that rebuilding the settlement was more important than gold prospecting. But out of respect for Newport, who had saved his life, he kept his objections to himself. Meanwhile, many of the newly arrived settlers, unprepared for the harsh conditions of life in the wilderness, became ill and died.

Weeks were wasted as Newport's gold-hungry men did nothing but search for the precious metal. Smith was disgusted by this useless activity, which delayed the spring planting. In a fit of anger he wrote that there was "no talke, no hope, no worke, but dig gold, wash gold, refine gold, loade gold." The gold hunters found nothing but worthless, glittering rocks. Finally, on April

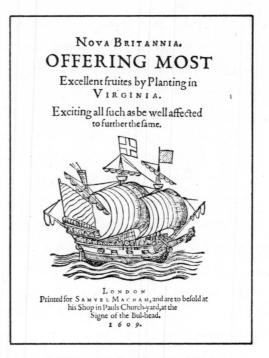

NOVA BRITANNIA.

OFFERING MOST

Excellent fruites by Planting in
VIRGINIA.

Exciting all such as be well affected
to further the same.

LONDON
Printed for SAMVEL MACHAM, and are to be sold at
his Shop in Pauls Church-yard, at the
Signe of the Bul-head.
1609.

*The title page from a
1609 booklet promoting
emigration to Virginia.*

10, Newport set sail for England. His three-month stay had accomplished little, except to use up much of the colony's limited food supply.

With the coming of warmer weather, things began to look up. At the end of April, another ship, the *Phoenix,* arrived, bringing much-needed supplies and forty more settlers. Prodded by Smith, the colonists cleared land and planted crops. When the *Phoenix* sailed for home in June, the colony seemed to be in good shape. The *Phoenix* carried a long letter from Smith to a friend in England. The letter was published later that year under the title *A True Relation of Such Occurrences and Accidents of Noate as*

Hath Hapned in Virginia. It was the beginning of Captain Smith's career as an author.

In the summer Smith went exploring again. His first voyage took him across Chesapeake Bay and up the Potomac River, where Smith observed that the woods "were extreme thick full of wolves, bears, deer and other wild beasts." During a brief stopover at Jamestown, Smith found the settlers in a rebellious mood. They were angry at President Ratcliffe for using up too much of the food supply and for putting men to work building a house for his personal use. Ratcliffe was deposed and Matthew Scrivener temporarily replaced him.

Resuming his explorations, Smith went as far north as the head of the Susquehanna River, near the border of what is now Pennsylvania. By the time he returned to Jamestown in early September he had thoroughly explored Chesapeake Bay and the major rivers emptying into it. The information he gathered enabled him to draw an excellent map of the region's principal features.

On September 10, 1608, three days after his return, Smith was elected president of the council. It was a tribute to his leadership ability, which virtually all of the colonists had come to respect. President Smith was to prove himself by far the ablest of the colony's early leaders. He quickly began a program to improve the settlement's defenses. The fort was repaired and enlarged and every man was required to drill regularly.

In October, Captain Newport returned with seventy new settlers. Among them were the colony's first women, Mrs. Thomas Forrest, the wife of one of the colonists, and her maid, Ann Burras. Soon the colony had its first wedding, when Ann married a carpenter named John Laydon. Newport also brought a group of "skillful workers from foreign parts." The workers were Dutchmen and Poles sent by the London Company to make pitch, tar, glass, and other items that could be exported for profit. Newport had firm orders from the London Company "not to return without a lump of gold," or information about a passage to the Pacific. Furthermore, to ensure friendship with the Indians, he was to crown Powhatan emperor in a formal ceremony.

First came the coronation of Chief Powhatan. Accompanied by fifty soldiers, Newport and Smith traveled overland to Powhatan's village. They brought with them gifts, including a bed with furnishings and fine silk clothes. At first suspicious, Powhatan was finally persuaded to put on a scarlet robe. But when he was asked to kneel so he could be crowned, he refused. Smith and Newport gently pushed him down just enough so that a copper crown could be placed on his head. Powhatan responded by presenting Newport with his deerskin robe and his old moccasins.

While Newport sailed upriver to explore, Smith supervised the production of small quantities of pitch, tar, glass, and soap ashes (wood ashes used to make lye). A party of men led by Smith cut down trees and made clapboard. By the time Newport returned, Smith had a full cargo ready for loading. Newport's expedition up the James had been a failure. No gold was found, nor any passage to the western sea.

In December, Newport sailed back to England, with the samples provided by Smith. He also took the troublesome and unpopular Ratcliffe, and a letter from Smith to the London Council. The letter, which Smith frankly called his "Rude Reply," sharply criticized the London Company's policies. He also complained about the type of settler being sent over. "When you send again I entreat you rather send but thirty carpenters, husbandmen, gardeners, blacksmiths, masons, and diggers up of trees . . . than a thousand such as we have."

A TIME OF
TROUBLE

The winter of 1608–1609 found the colony once again facing a serious food shortage. Smith's immediate task was to feed two hundred hungry settlers. But Powhatan, hoping to starve the English out of his land, had ordered his tribes not to sell corn to the settlers. However, Smith was determined to get the supplies he needed. Taking forty-six volunteers in three small boats, he made his way to Powhatan's village. Smith and his men arrived there on January 12, 1609. Powhatan did not seem happy to see Smith, even though he had earlier sent word for him to come.

When they sat down to trade, Powhatan demanded swords and muskets in exchange for corn. Smith refused, saying, "I told you long ago I had none to spare." A long bargaining session followed. In spite of their claims of friendship, each suspected the other of treachery. While the trading was going on, Powhatan suddenly left the lodge. Moments later a band of warriors surrounded the house. Smith fired his pistol to frighten them off. Then he ordered his men to train their muskets on other Indians who were bringing baskets of corn. At gunpoint, Smith forced them to load his boat.

Not enough corn had been obtained from Powhatan, so Smith sailed along the river to other Indian villages. By threatening to destroy their homes, Smith forced the Indians to give him the corn he needed. Smith got the corn, but bad blood remained between Indians and whites. Many of his critics later accused Smith of dealing too harshly with the Indians. It is true that he followed a hard line, believing it the only way to keep the colony alive. But his tactics were mild compared to those of his successors, who brutally massacred Indian women and children.

Returning to Jamestown with nearly 500 bushels of corn and other provisions, Smith learned that the remaining councilors had died. He was now completely in charge of the colony. Ruling with an iron hand, Smith put every man to work—gentlemen included. There would be no more shirkers at Jamestown. His tough policy toward idlers was summed up in the statement "He that will not worke shall not eate."

From February to May, the colony bustled with activity. An additional forty acres of land was cleared and readied for planting corn. Twenty new houses were constructed, and a blockhouse was built on the narrow neck connecting the island to the mainland. Inside the fort, a deep well was dug, providing the settlers "with excellent sweet water, which till then was wanting." Hogs and chickens were raised. In all, it was a good time for the colony.

But disaster was never far off. While the settlers were busying themselves with all these projects, the supply of corn was left unattended. Rats got into the sheds and ate most of the precious food supply. To deal with the new crisis, Smith ordered the settlers to go out to live wherever they could find food. His prompt action saved most of the colonists from starvation.

A TRAGIC
ACCIDENT

In July, a ship arrived bringing food and important news. A new charter had been granted to the London Company by King James. John Smith's "Rude Reply" had set the company leaders to thinking. The charter of 1609 provided for changes in the colony's government. In place of the council, with its constant feuding, the colony was to be ruled by "one able and absolute governor." The company had also decided to follow Smith's advice to wait for profits and first build up the settlement. It advertised throughout England for more settlers, offering them shares of stock and tracts of land in Virginia.

Nine ships crowded with five hundred eager settlers set sail from England in June. Storms and disease took their toll, however. Near Bermuda, the ships were lashed by a hurricane. One vessel sank, and the flagship, carrying the colony's new lieutenant governor, Sir Thomas Gates, ran aground and was wrecked. The surviving ships straggled into Jamestown in August. To his dismay, Smith discovered among the new arrivals his old enemies Ratcliffe and Archer. Having denounced Smith before the London Council, they now plotted to remove him from office.

But Smith had more important problems to worry about. The settlement was now burdened by four hundred demoralized and fever-ridden newcomers. It was too late in the season to plant fresh crops of corn. To ease the overcrowding, Smith encouraged groups of colonists to move out of the fort and establish new settlements. Soon after, Smith visited one of these settlements to see how it was coming along. On his way back, someone carelessly set fire to his gunpowder bag. The flashing powder badly burned his thighs and body. His comrades brought their seriously injured commander back to Jamestown.

Ratcliffe and Archer saw their opportunity. They deposed Smith and put George Percy in his place until the new governor, Lord De La Warr, arrived. Smith was put on board a ship bound for England. His enemies drew up charges against him to be presented to the London Council. They accused him of bad leadership, of causing trouble with the Indians, and of plotting to marry Pocahontas and become king.

On this unpleasant note, John Smith's short and stormy career at Jamestown came to an end. There is no question that his actions saved the colony. But as a leader, he had many shortcomings. A man of action rather than ideas, he was recklessly brave but not always wise. His quick temper often led him to speak and act rashly. Virginius Dabney, in his *Virginia: The New Dominion*, has observed: "[Smith] had been unsparing and often unfair in his criticisms of the other leaders, and they had been similarly critical of him. . . . [Yet] it was he, more than any other man, who pulled Jamestown through the worst crises of its early years."

It was unfortunate that Smith left the colony when he did. His services were sorely needed in the months that followed. As cold weather approached, the Indians became hostile. They had learned that the settlers were weakest in winter and so they refused to provide corn and other food. The winter of 1609–1610 became known as the "Starving Time." Of five hundred settlers, barely sixty survived. George Percy, Smith's successor, described how the colonists ate "dogs, cats, rats, and mice"—even boots and shoes—"to satisfy cruel hunger."

When Sir Thomas Gates, the new lieutenant governor, finally arrived on May 22, 1610, he found the sick and hungry survivors in complete despair. Conditions were so bad it was decided to abandon the colony. The remaining settlers boarded Gates's two ships and headed down the James River. They had not gone far, however, when word reached them that Lord De La Warr (Delaware) was on his way with fresh provisions and another batch of settlers. De La Warr's timely arrival saved the Jamestown settlement.

Within a few years, new life had been breathed into the Virginia colony. Around 1612, the colonists began to grow tobacco as a cash crop. Soon thousands of pounds were being exported to England. Tobacco turned out to be a substitute for the gold the early settlers had sought. It enabled the colony to thrive and expand, and gave its London backers the profits they craved.

A MAN WITH
A MISSION

While all this was taking place, Smith was back in London defending himself against the charges made by his Jamestown enemies. He had to account for his actions before the company's London Council, and apparently a trial of some sort was held. What took place at this trial is not known, since the company records for this period have been lost. But surely Captain Smith had a few choice words for the aristocratic gentlemen who sat as his judges.

There is no record of any sentence being imposed on Smith, so we may assume that the charges were eventually dropped. Nevertheless, Smith was unhappy about the damage to his reputation. He spent the next two years trying to clear his name. As part of this effort, he assembled a great deal of material defending his management of the colony, which was published in his book *A Map of Virginia. With a Description of the Countrey*. The book came out in 1612 and included a description of the Virginia territory, its resources, and the customs and way of life of the Indians. Smith's map of Virginia was so highly thought of that it remained in use for nearly two centuries.

But Smith was not just an angry man out to right the wrongs he felt had been done to him. Virginia and the New World had fired his imagination. He had become a man with a mission. The rest of his life was to be spent promoting English settlement of North America. As he would later write, America was a land where someone with little money and "only his merit to advance his fortunes" could start a new life.

Smith wanted very much to return to America. Because of his trouble with the London Company, he could not go back to southern Virginia. Nevertheless, the northern region (present-day New England), which had been granted to the Plymouth Company, was still open to him.

To get there, however, he needed backing. This he was able to obtain from some London merchants. By promising to search for whales, gold, and copper, he persuaded them to put up money for two ships. Early in 1614, Smith put out to sea. In April, he reached the coast of Maine and established a base at Monhegan

NEW ENGLAND 1614

Androscoggin R.

Sagadahoc (Kennebec) R.

Penobscot

Monhegan Is.

Cape Elizabeth

Merrimack R.

Cape Ann

Charles R.

ATLANTIC

OCEAN

Plymouth

Cape James (Cape Cod)

Stuards Bay (Cape Cod Bay)

Capawack (Martha's Vineyard)

10   20   30   40   50

Scale of miles

WKP.

A

DESCRIPTION

of *New England*:

OR

THE OBSERVATIONS, AND
difcoueries, of Captain *Iohn Smith* (Admirall
of that Country) in the North of *America*, in the year
of our Lord 1614: *with the fucceffe of fixe Ships,*
that went the next yeare 1615; *and the*
accidents befell him among the
French men of warre:

With the proofe of the prefent benefit this
Countrey affoords: whither this prefent yeare,
1616, *eight voluntary Ships are gone*
to make further tryall.

At LONDON
Printed by *Humfrey Lownes*, for *Robert Clerke*; and
are to be fould at his houfe called the Lodge,
in Chancery lane, ouer againft Lin-
colnes Inne. 1616.

The title page from A Description
of New England *by Captain John Smith.*
It is the earliest book in which
the name "New England" occurs.

Island. His main purpose was to hunt for whales. "We saw many and spent much time in chasing them," he reported, "but could not kill any." The search for gold also proved futile.

Still, there was wealth to be found in the sea. Smith had his men catch and dry fish to bring back to England. But fishing was not his kind of work. Ever the explorer, he went off in a small boat with eight men. The rugged coast of Maine did not appeal to him. Massachusetts, on the other hand, was in his eyes "the Paradise of all those parts." He was enchanted by this fertile region—which he named "New England"—and thought that it would be an ideal place for future settlements.

Most of his time was spent mapping the coast and trading with the Indians for beaver and otter skins. By mid-July he was ready to sail home. He brought back a cargo of dried fish and valuable furs. Having richly rewarded his backers, Smith found it easier to get support for another voyage. Sir Ferdinando Gorges, a prominent member of the Northern Virginia (or Plymouth) Company, threw his weight behind Smith's proposed New England settlement. In March 1615, Smith again set sail for New England, hoping to establish a colony that would support itself by fishing and fur trading. Unfortunately, a storm struck Smith's ship with such fury that it snapped all three of the vessel's masts.

Forced to return to Plymouth, Smith persuaded his backers to provide him with another ship. With his small band of colonists, Smith sailed from Plymouth at the end of June, only to run into more bad luck. A few days after leaving port, he was captured by pirates. During his captivity, he began to write *A Description of New England*, the first full account of the region and its resources. Eventually he escaped from the pirates and made his way back to Plymouth.

ADMIRAL OF
NEW ENGLAND

Smith arrived in Plymouth in December 1615. From there he went to London, where he spent the next months working on his map of New England and arranging for the publication of his manuscript. The book, which came out in the summer of 1616, was a plea for the settlement of this bountiful territory. He correctly predicted that fishing would be the main economic activity. New England's "silvered streams" of fish, he maintained, would be a source of riches as great as the gold of Spain's New World possessions. The engraved map of New England that appeared in the book was the most accurate made up to that time.

Unfortunately, the book did not cause much of a stir when it was first published. However, several years later it inspired the Pilgrims, a group of religious nonconformists, to choose Massachusetts as the place to found a settlement. Smith offered to go with the group and serve as a guide. But according to the captain, the thrifty Pilgrims turned him down, "saying my books and maps were much better cheape to teach them than myselfe." So the Pilgrims went off to found the Plymouth colony (1620), while a restless Captain Smith remained in England.

The success of the Pilgrims gave a boost to Smith's advertisements for New England. In recognition of his work on behalf of the area, the Plymouth Company appointed him "Admiral of

New England." But Smith was an admiral in name only, for he never got a fleet to go with the title. His later attempts to return to New England were frustrated. Still, his tireless efforts to open up this region to English settlement was one of his major accomplishments. As the noted historian Samuel Eliot Morison put it, ". . . few of her founders gave to New England so much, and got so little, as Captain John Smith."

FINAL YEARS

Denied an opportunity to return to the America he loved, Smith now devoted himself to his writing. He became a full-time author and historian. In 1620 he published *New England Trials*, which was revised in 1622 to include an account of the Pilgrim settlement at Plymouth. Two years later he produced a more ambitious work, *The Generall Historie of Virgina, New-England, and the Summer Isles*. In it he traced the history of English exploration and settlement of North America from the Cabot voyages to his own day. Much of the book dealt with his experiences as a colonist and explorer.

Next he wrote *An Accidence or The Path-way to Experience* (1626), which was a handbook on seamanship. A larger version of this book, called *The Seaman's Grammar*, was issued

A portrait of Captain John Smith as he is shown on his own map of New England first published in 1614. Below, Captain John Smith's coat of arms.

in 1627. By 1629 he had completed his *True Travels,* which was published the following year. But to the end of his days, America was constantly on his mind. His last book, brought out in 1631, was entitled *Advertisements For the unexperienced Planters of New England.*

John Smith's dream was to see a great British empire hacked out of the forests of North America. He would not live to see it, but it did come about. Jamestown and the settlement of New England were the beginnings of that empire, and Captain Smith played an important part in both. Because of this, some historians rank Smith high on the list of Britain's most notable empire builders.

Toward the end of his life, Smith fell on hard times. He spent his last years in London, and it was said of him that he had "a prince's mind imprisoned in a poor man's purse." Yet he never faced real poverty. Smith had many prominent and wealthy friends who came to his aid. One of these was Sir Samuel Saltonstall, who held the post of Collector of the Customs. Smith was living in Sir Samuel's home when he died, at the age of fifty-one, on June 21, 1631. He was buried in Saint Sepulchre's Church, just outside the old city wall.

Inscribed on Captain Smith's coat of arms was a Latin expression, *Vincere est vivere.* It means "To overcome is to live." Smith's whole life was spent living up to that motto. He struggled to lift himself up by his own efforts from commoner to gentleman; he fought and conquered his enemies on many battlefields; he helped to overcome a hostile wilderness, and by his common sense and bold leadership kept alive the fragile Jamestown settlement. His life was a constant struggle to overcome—to achieve. In a sense, he even overcame death, for Captain John Smith lives on in history and in legend.

A NOTE
ON SOURCES

Anyone writing about Captain John Smith must start with his own works, which have been conveniently gathered in a single edition entitled *Travels and Works of Captain John Smith*, edited by Edward Arber and A. G. Bradley. Of particular interest to the biographer are Smith's *True Travels* and his *Generall Historie of Virginia*, previously cited in this book. Among recent biographies, *Captain John Smith: His Life and Legend* by Bradford Smith and *The Three Worlds of Captain John Smith* by Philip Barbour proved most useful.

Additional information about the early years of the Jamestown settlement may be found in *Virginia: The New Dominion* by Virginius Dabney. An excellent summary of Smith's New England explorations and promotional activities is contained in *Builders of The Bay Colony* by Samuel Eliot Morison.

Author's note: Most of the quotations from contemporary sources have been put into modern English so as not to confuse the reader. Occasionally, however, the original old English spelling of words has been retained for dramatic effect.

INDEX

THE AUTHOR

Henry Ira Kurtz, a graduate of Columbia University, has also studied at Oxford University and the University of Vienna. He is an editor and writer whose articles have appeared in *History Today*, *American History Illustrated*, and other periodicals. He is the author of the Visual Biography *John and Sebastian Cabot*.